step
japanese
and korean
cooking

PERIPLUS

GLOSSARY

Daikon: Large white radish used a great deal in Japan. Served grated or thinly sliced as a garnish, or pickled in a solution of soy sauce and sugar. Available fresh, or packaged as a pickle.

Dashi: Basic stock in Japanese cuisine. Made with dried kelp and dried bonito (a fish). Available in packaged forms—ground, as granules or in flakes—simply add hot water to make up stock.

Hot Bean Paste: Also called chilli bean paste and used extensively in Korean cooking. Made from chilli, soya beans, garlic and flavourings. Commercial paste can be extremely hot, so use with caution.

Mirin: A mild, low-alcohol form of *sake*, this cooking rice wine lends sweetness to sauces, grilled dishes and glazes.

Miso: Fermented soya bean paste, a staple of the Japanese diet. Available in many varieties including light brown, red, brown, yellow and white, each differing in flavour and texture. Used in soups, sauces, marinades and dips.

Nori: The most common form of dried seaweed used by the Japanese and Koreans. It comes in sheets or soft shreds, plain or roasted (for a more palatable flavour). Additional quick toasting over a naked flame freshens the nori and produces a nutty flavour.

Pickled Ginger: Fresh, thin, pink or bright red slices of ginger in a brine. Used in rice dishes and as a garnish. A good palate cleanser with a very sharp flavour.

Rice Vinegar: A mild, sweet, delicate-flavoured vinegar made from rice.

Sake: Rice wine, available for cooking or drinking. Cooking sake has a lower alcohol content.

Sansho: A delicious seasoning unique to Japan and China. Often sprinkled on meat.

Sesame and Seaweed Sprinkle: A combination of finely chopped nori, roasted sesame seeds and salt. Sprinkle on noodles, salads and egg dishes.

Sesame Seeds: Black and white sesame seeds are used in Japanese and Korean cooking. Full-flavoured and plump, the seeds may be bought already toasted and can be ground before using.

Shichimi Togarashi: A seven-spice condiment, used as a seasoning and for sprinkling on soups and noodles.

Soba: Noodles made from buckwheat flour and available dried, and sometimes fresh, from Asian speciality stores.

Soy Sauce (Japanese): Called *shoyu* and much lighter and sweeter than Chinese soy sauce. Naturally brewed, so refrigerate after opening.

Tempura Flour: A very light flour, available from Japanese food speciality stores, that gives batter a light, bubbly texture.

Tofu: Milky-white soya bean curd, available in very firm or soft (silken) blocks. With a subtle taste, tofu absorbs the flavours of spices and sauces. An excellent source of protein.

Tonkatsu Sauce: A tasty barbecue-style sauce made with tomatoes, apples, Japanese Worcestershire sauce and mustard. Usually served with breaded fried pork.

Wasabi: A pungent paste made from the root of the wasabi (horseradish) plant. It is extremely hot, so use with discretion. It is available as a powder or a paste.

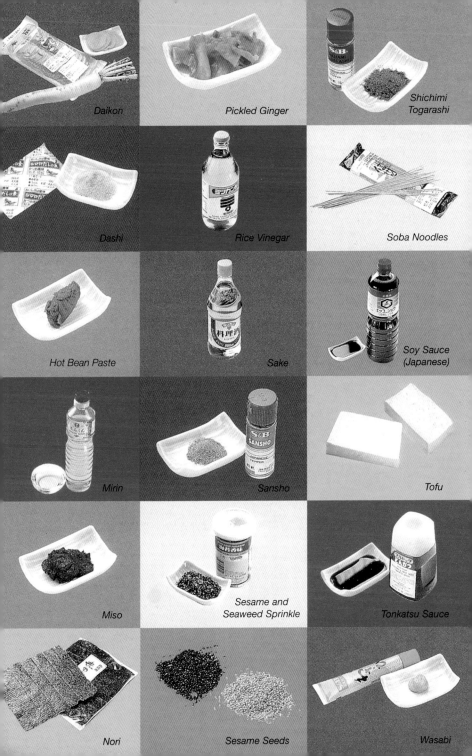

Daikon

Pickled Ginger

Shichimi
Togarashi

Dashi

Rice Vinegar

Soba Noodles

Hot Bean Paste

Sake

Soy Sauce
(Japanese)

Mirin

Sansho

Tofu

Miso

Sesame and
Seaweed Sprinkle

Tonkatsu Sauce

Nori

Sesame Seeds

Wasabi

To toast sesame seeds, place in a small dry pan; toss over low heat until golden.

Halve the cucumber, and then use a teaspoon to remove any seeds.

JAPANESE

*Given the mystique surrounding this unique cuisine, it's surprising
how easy it is to prepare once you know how.*

Sunomono

Prawn salad served
in a piquant dressing.

Preparation time:
20 minutes
+ 1 hour marinating
Total cooking time:
5 minutes
Serves 4

---

*½ telegraph cucumber
375 g (12 oz)
medium raw prawns
¼ cup (60 ml/2 fl oz)
rice vinegar
1 tablespoon caster
sugar*

*1 tablespoon soy
sauce
1 teaspoon finely
grated fresh ginger
1 tablespoon toasted
sesame seeds*

---

1. Halve cucumber
lengthways and
remove any seeds
with a teaspoon;
remove skin with a
vegetable peeler. Cut
flesh into thin slices,
sprinkle thoroughly
with salt and set aside
for 5 minutes. Rinse
to remove salt; pat dry
with paper towels.
2. Place the prawns in
a pan of lightly salted
boiling water and
simmer for 2 minutes,
or until just cooked.
Drain and plunge
them into cold water.
Allow the prawns to
cool and then peel
and devein them,
leaving tails intact.
3. Place the vinegar,
sugar, soy sauce and
ginger in a large bowl
and stir until the sugar
dissolves. Add the
prawns and cucumber
and marinate 1 hour.
4. Arrange on serving
plates, sprinkle with
seeds and serve.
Note: These raw or
lightly cooked foods,
marinated and served
in a vinegared
dressing, are a
delicious appetizer.

*Rinse the cucumber slices, then pat dry
with paper towels.*

*Peel and devein the cooked prawns,
leaving the tails intact.*

Tofu Miso Soup

A nourishing staple.

Preparation time:
15 minutes
Total cooking time:
7 minutes
Serves 4

250 g (8 oz) tofu	*1/2 cup (80 g/2²/3 oz)*
1 spring onion	*dashi grains*
4 cups (1 litre)	*100 g (3¹/3 oz) miso*
water	*1 tablespoon mirin*

1. Use a sharp knife to cut the tofu into cubes. Slice the spring onion diagonally into 1 cm (¹/2 inch) lengths. Set tofu and onion aside.

2. Using a wooden spoon, combine the water and dashi in a small pan, then bring the mixture to the boil. Combine the miso and mirin in a small bowl, then add to the boiling liquid in the pan. Stir the miso over medium heat, taking care not to let the mixture boil once the miso has dissolved (overheating will result in the loss of miso flavour).

3. Add the tofu cubes to the hot stock and heat, without boiling, over medium heat for 5 minutes.

4. Serve in individual soup bowls, garnished with the spring onion.

Use a sharp knife to carefully cut the tofu into 1 cm (¹/2 inch) cubes.

Carefully slice the spring onion into 1 cm (¹/2 inch) diagonals.

Stirring with a wooden spoon, combine the water with the dashi in a small pan.

Place the miso and the mirin in a small bowl and mix until well combined.

Sushi Rolls

Savoury rice treats.

Preparation time:
45 minutes
Total cooking time:
8–10 minutes
Makes about 30

---

1 cup (220 g/7 oz)
short-grain
white rice
2 cups (500 ml/
16 fl oz) water
2 tablespoons rice
vinegar
1 tablespoon caster
sugar
1 teaspoon salt
4 sheets nori

wasabi, to taste
125 g (4 oz) smoked
salmon, trout or
fresh sashimi tuna
1 small Lebanese
cucumber, peeled
1/2 small avocado,
optional
3 tablespoons pickled
ginger or vegetables
soy sauce, for dipping

---

1. Wash the rice in cold water until the water runs clear; drain thoroughly. Place the rice and water in a medium pan. Bring to the boil, then reduce the heat and simmer, uncovered, for 4–5 minutes, or until all the water is absorbed. Cover and reduce the heat to very low and cook for another 4–5 minutes. Remove the pan from the heat and cool, covered, for about 10 minutes.
2. Add the combined vinegar, sugar and salt to the rice, tossing with a wooden spoon until the rice is cool.
3. Place one sheet of nori on a piece of greaseproof paper, or bamboo mat, on a flat surface; pat a quarter of the rice along one long side of the nori, leaving a 2 cm (1 inch) border around the remaining three sides. Spread a very small amount of wasabi down the centre of the rice. Cut the fish into thin strips. Cut the cucumber and avocado into matchsticks about

5 cm (2 inches) in length. Arrange a quarter of the pieces of fish, cucumber, avocado and ginger or vegetables on top of the wasabi stripe.
4. Using the paper or mat as a guide, roll nori up firmly from the bottom, enclosing rice around centred ingredients. Press the nori edges together to seal the roll.
5. Using a sharp flat-bladed or electric knife, cut the roll into 2.5 cm (1 inch) rounds. Repeat with remaining ingredients. Serve sushi on individual small plates with small bowls of soy sauce and extra wasabi (to be mixed to make a dipping sauce).
Note: Sushi Rolls can be made up to 4 hours in advance and kept, covered, in the refrigerator. Slice into pieces just before serving. Sashimi tuna is available from good fishmongers — make sure the fish is extremely fresh.

Boil the rice until the water is absorbed, then cover and reduce the heat.

Place one quarter of the rice along one side of each nori sheet.

Commencing at the bottom, roll the nori up to enclose the rice and filling.

Use a sharp knife to cut the sushi roll into 2.5 cm (1 inch) rounds.

Yakitori (Skewered Chicken)

Preparation time:
20 minutes + soaking
Total cooking time:
10 minutes
Makes about
25 skewers

---

1 kg (2 lb) chicken thigh fillets
1/2 cup (125 ml/ 4 fl oz) sake
3/4 cup (185 ml/6 fl oz) dark soy sauce

1/2 cup (125 ml/ 4 fl oz) mirin
2 tablespoons sugar
1 cup (65 g/2 1/4 oz) spring onions, cut 2 cm (3/4 inch) diagonally

---

1. Soak 25 wooden skewers for about 20 minutes in water; drain and set aside.

2. Cut the chicken fillets into bite-sized pieces. Combine the sake, soy sauce, mirin and sugar in a small pan. Bring to the boil, then set aside.

3. Thread the chicken pieces onto wooden skewers alternately with the spring onions. Place skewers on a foil-lined tray; cook under a preheated grill, turning and brushing frequently with the sauce, 7–8 minutes, or until the chicken is cooked through.

Use a sharp knife to cut the chicken into bite-sized pieces.

Combine the sake, soy sauce, mirin and sugar in a small pan.

Thread the chicken pieces and spring onions alternately onto the skewers.

Brush the kebabs frequently with the sauce as they cook.

Sashimi (Raw Sliced Fish)

Preparation time:
30 minutes
Total cooking time:
nil
Serves 4

500 g (1 lb) very fresh fish such as tuna, salmon, kingfish, ocean trout, snapper, whiting bream or jewfish

Japanese soy sauce, to serve
wasabi, to serve
1 carrot, peeled
1 daikon, peeled

1. Use a very sharp, flat-bladed knife to remove any skin from the fish. Place the fish in the freezer. Chill until the fish is just firm enough to be cut thinly and evenly into slices, about 5 mm (¼ inch) in width. Cut with an even motion, taking care not to saw.

2. Arrange the sashimi pieces attractively on a platter. Traditionally served with Japanese soy sauce and wasabi.
3. Use a zester to scrape carrot and daikon into long fine strips or, alternatively, cut them into fine julienne strips. Garnish with the carrot and daikon.

Use a very sharp flat-bladed knife to remove the skin from the fish.

Cut the fish into even slices, about 5 mm (¼ inch) thick, taking care not to saw.

For garnishing, use a zester to scrape long thin strips of carrot and daikon.

As an alternative garnish, cut the daikon and carrot into fine julienne strips.

Prawn Tempura

Delicate morsels.

Preparation time:
40 minutes
Total cooking time:
15 minutes
Serves 4

20 large raw prawns	*1¹/4 cups (155 g/*
1 sheet nori	*5 oz) tempura flour*
flour, for coating	*or light (cake) flour*
1 cup (250 ml/	*2 egg yolks*
8 fl oz) iced water	*oil, for deep-frying*

1. Shell and devein prawns, leaving tails intact. Cut 4 incisions in the undersection of each prawn, then straighten out to open up the cuts. Cut the nori into strips and wrap a piece around base of tail of each prawn. Seal with a touch of water.

2. Coat the prawns lightly with flour, leaving the seaweed and tail uncoated. Combine the water tempura flour and yolks; mix lightly and use at once (the batter will be lumpy).

3. Heat the oil in a deep pan. Dip each prawn into the batter, leaving the tail and seaweed uncoated; fry quickly in the hot oil. Remove when just golden; drain on paper towels. Serve at once.

Carefully cut four incisions into the undersection of each prawn.

Wrap the nori strips around the base of the tail of each prawn.

Combine the flour, water and egg yolks in a bowl to make a batter.

Dip each prawn in the batter, then quickly fry in the hot oil.

Teppan yaki (Grilled Steak and Vegetables)

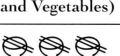

Preparation time:
45 minutes
Total cooking time:
approx 25 minutes
Serves 4

---

350 g (11¼ oz)
scotch fillet,
partially frozen
4 small ladyfinger
eggplants
100 g (3⅓ oz) fresh
shiitake mushrooms
100 g (3⅓ oz) baby
green beans
6 baby yellow or
green squash
1 red or green
capsicum, seeded

6 spring onions,
outside layer
removed
210 g (6¾ oz)
canned bamboo
shoots, drained
¼ cup (60 ml/2 fl oz)
light vegetable oil
soy and ginger
dipping sauce or
sesame seed
dipping sauce
(pages 32–33)

---

1. Slice the steak into very thin pieces (this is very easy to do if the steak is partially frozen). Mark a large cross on each slice of meat. Place the slices in a single layer on a large serving platter and season thoroughly with plenty of salt and freshly ground pepper. Set the meat aside while the vegetables are being prepared.
2. Trim ends from the eggplants and cut the flesh into long, very thin diagonal slices. Trim any hard stems from the mushrooms, and top and tail the beans. If the beans are longer than about 7 cm (2¾ inches), cut them in two. Quarter or halve the squash, or leave whole, depending on the size. Cut the capsicum into thin strips and slice the spring onions into lengths about 7 cm (2¾ inches)

long, discarding the tops. Trim the bamboo shoot slices to a similar size. Arrange all the vegetables attractively in separate bundles on a serving plate.
3. When the guests are seated, heat an electric grill or electric frying pan until very hot, and then lightly brush it with the oil. Quickly fry about a quarter of the meat, searing on both sides, and then push it over to the edge of the pan. Add about a quarter of the vegetables to the grill or pan and quickly stir-fry, adding a little more oil as needed. Serve a small portion of the meat and vegetables to guests in individual servings. The food should be dipped into a sauce of their choice, and then eaten. Serve with steamed rice.
4. Repeat the process with the remaining meat and vegetables, cooking in small batches as extra helpings are requested.

16

Use a large sharp knife to slice the steak into very thin slices.

Using the same knife, make a large cross on each slice of meat.

Carefully trim any hard stems from the fresh shiitake mushrooms.

Sear the meat quickly on each side, using tongs to turn it.

Tonkatsu (Crumbed Fried Pork)

Preparation time:
35 minutes +
2 hours refrigeration
Total cooking time:
12 minutes
Serves 4

---

500 g (1 lb) pork loin
good pinch each salt and pepper
1/2 cup (60 g/2 oz) plain flour
6 egg yolks, beaten with 2 tablespoons water
2 cups (120 g/4 oz) Japanese dried breadcrumbs
2 spring onions

pickled ginger and pickled daikon
2 cups (90 g/3 oz) finely shredded Chinese or Savoy cabbage
1 sheet nori
1 1/2 cups (375 ml/ 12 fl oz) oil, for frying
1 cup (250 ml/8 fl oz) Tonkatsu sauce

---

1. Trim pork of any sinew and cut into 8 thin slices. Sprinkle the slices with the salt and pepper and lightly coat with flour.

2. Dip each steak into the egg mixture and then in breadcrumbs; press the crumbs on with your fingertips to ensure an even coating. Place the steaks in a single layer on a plate and refrigerate, uncovered, for at least 2 hours.

3. Meanwhile, prepare the garnishes. Peel away the outside layers of the spring onions, then slice the stems very finely and place in a bowl of cold water until serving time. Slice the ginger and daikon and set aside with the shredded cabbage. Using a sharp knife, shred the nori very finely and then break into strips about 4 cm (1 1/2 inches)

long. Set strips aside until serving time.

4. Heat the oil in a heavy-based frying pan until hot. Cook 2–3 steaks at a time until golden brown on both sides, then drain on kitchen paper. Repeat the process with the remaining steaks. Carefully slice the steaks into 1 cm (1/2 inch) strips and reassemble into the original steak shape. Top each of the steaks with a small bundle of the nori strips. Serve with the Tonkatsu sauce, shredded cabbage, drained spring onions, pickled ginger, daikon and steamed rice.

Note: Japanese breadcrumbs give an authentic, extremely light and delicious coating to this dish — use either the fine or coarse variety as both will give excellent results. Always store Tonkatsu sauce in the refrigerator after opening.

Use your fingertips to press the crumbs onto the pork.

Slice the ginger and daikon finely and set aside with the shredded cabbage.

Shred the nori finely, and then break it into strips about 4 cm (1½ inches) long.

Cook 2–3 steaks at a time until golden brown on both sides.

Sukiyaki

The famous 'hot-pot'.

Preparation time:
60 minutes
Total cooking time:
15 minutes
Serves 6

---

500 g (1 lb) scotch
fillet, partially
frozen
3 small white onions,
peeled
5 spring onions,
peeled
1 large carrot, peeled
400 g (12²/₃ oz)
small button
mushrooms, stalks
trimmed
1/2 small Chinese
cabbage
100 g (3¹/₃ oz) firm
tofu
2 cups (180 g/5³/₄oz)
bean sprouts
225 g (7¹/₄ oz)
canned bamboo
shoots, drained

100 g (3¹/₃ oz)
Japanese Sukiyaki
noodles (see Note)
6 eggs

SAUCE
1/3 cup (80 ml/
2³/₄ fl oz) Japanese
soy sauce
1/4 cup (60 ml/
2 fl oz) light beef
stock
1/4 cup (60 ml/
2 fl oz) sake
1/4 cup (60 ml/
2 fl oz) mirin
2 tablespoons caster
sugar
1/4 cup (60 ml/
2 fl oz) vegetable oil

---

1. Using an extremely
sharp knife, slice the
slightly frozen fillet as
thinly as possible,
then arrange the
slices attractively on a
large tray or platter,
leaving room for the
ready-to-cook assort-
ment of tofu, noodles
and vegetables. Cover
the fillet slices and
refrigerate the platter
while preparing the
remaining ingredients.
2. Cut each of the
white onions into
6 wedges. Slice the
white bottoms and the
firm section of the

green tops of the spring onions into 4 cm (1¹/2 inch) lengths and discard the remainder. Cut the carrot into matchsticks of similar length to the spring onions; wipe the mushrooms over with a clean cloth, then cut them in half. Discarding any tough outer leaves and stalk, cut the cabbage into bite-sized pieces. Cut the tofu into bite-sized cubes measuring about 2 cm (³/4 inch). Trim and discard the straggly ends from the bean sprouts, and slice the bamboo shoots into even-sized pieces. Arrange all the vegetables and tofu on the platter

with the meat slices.

3. Parboil the noodles for 2–5 minutes or until just soft; do not overcook or they can dissolve. Drain thoroughly and, using scissors, cut the cooked noodles into approximately 5 cm (2 inch) lengths—just long enough so they can be picked up easily when using chopsticks. Arrange the noodles on the platter with the meat, vegetables and tofu.

4. To make Sauce: Combine the soy sauce, beef stock, sake, mirin and sugar in a small bowl and stir until the sugar is dissolved.

5. Just before serving, heat a large frying pan, or an electric

frying pan if cooking the Sukiyaki at the dining table, and brush lightly with oil. When the pan is very hot, take about one-third of the onions, spring onions, carrot, mushrooms, cabbage, bamboo shoots and tofu and cook quickly for about 2 minutes, tossing constantly but keeping them separate from one another as much as possible. Push the vegetables and tofu to the side of the pan. Add about one-third of the bean sprouts and noodles to the pan, gently toss for a minute, then push to one side with the other ingredients. Add about one-third of the meat slices in one layer and sear for

Trim the bamboo shoots into even-sized pieces, similar to the other vegetables.

Using scissors, cut the cooked noodles into short lengths.

30 seconds on each side, taking care not to overcook them. Spoon a little of the sauce over the meat, then toss them together until the meat is just browned through. Turn the heat down to low and gently toss all the ingredients together just prior to serving.

6. Sukiyaki should be served straight from the hot frying pan (or electric frying pan), placed in the centre of the table. Each diner breaks a raw egg into his or her individual soup bowl, whisking it with chopsticks, to use as a dipping medium. Using a pair of chopsticks, each diner picks up an individual mouthful of Sukiyaki and dips it in the beaten egg before eating.

7. When ready for second servings, the frying pan is heated to high again and the cooking process repeated. After all the solid ingredients of the Sukiyaki have been eaten, the delicious cooking liquid that remains, redolent with the ingredients' flavour, is eaten on its own, with steamed rice.

Note: The meat and vegetables should be cooked in batches, as required, to ensure that ingredients don't overcook. The recipe can be assembled to the end of step 4 up to 2 hours before cooking time. Make sure you have everything on the table and your guests comfortably seated before cooking commences.

There are two types of noodles that are normally used for Sukiyaki. *Harusame* are very fine, white noodles, almost transparent. They are similar to Chinese-style cellophane noodles, which can be used as a substitute. *Shirataki* noodles are translucent but jelly-like and are made from the root of the 'devil's tongue' plant. All these noodles are available from Asian food stores.

Some people prefer to have Sukiyaki on rice, even though it is not traditional.

Push the vegetables to one side of the pan, and then add one-third of the meat.

Spoon a little of the sauce over the cooked meat.

23

Deep-fried Chicken with Seaweed

Golden delight.

Preparation time:
25 minutes +
15 minutes
marinating
Total cooking time:
20 minutes
Serves 4

---

400 g (12²/₃ oz)
chicken breast
tenderloins
¼ cup (60 ml/
2 fl oz) Japanese
soy sauce
¼ cup (60 ml/
2 fl oz) mirin
4 cm (1½ inches)
ginger, very
finely grated

1 sheet nori, finely
chopped or
crumbled into very
small pieces
⅓ cup (40 g/
1⅓ oz) cornflour
1 cup (250 ml/
8 fl oz) vegetable
oil, for frying
pickled ginger and
thin cucumber slices

---

1. Carefully trim and discard any sinew from the chicken. Cut the chicken into bite-sized pieces and discard any thin ends so that pieces will be an even size. Place the chicken pieces in a bowl.

2. Combine the soy sauce, mirin and ginger in a small jug and pour the mixture over the chicken; toss until the pieces are evenly coated with the marinade. Set aside for 15 minutes, then drain off any excess marinade.

3. Mix the nori with the cornflour and, using your fingertips, lightly coat each piece of chicken in the cornflour mixture. Heat the oil in a heavy-based frying pan over medium heat. Fry 6–7 pieces at a time until golden, turning regularly. Drain on paper towels; serve with steamed rice, pickled ginger and sliced cucumber. Garnish with extra strips of nori, if desired.

Note: Use a very sharp knife or scissors to cut the nori.

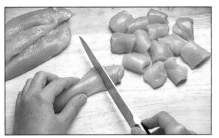

Cut the chicken tenderloins into bite-sized pieces.

Pour the combined soy sauce, mirin and ginger over the chicken.

Using your fingertips, lightly coat each
chicken piece with the cornflour mixture.

Fry 6–7 pieces at a time until golden
brown, then drain on paper towels.

Salted Grilled Fish

Preparation time:
25 minutes
Total cooking time:
approx 18 minutes
Serves 4

---

400 g (12²/₃ oz)
small whole bream,
whiting or snapper,
cleaned, scaled
with eyes removed
(see Note)
½ lemon, cut into
thin slices
5 cm (2 inches) very
fresh ginger
1 tablespoon mirin

2 tablespoons
Japanese soy sauce
3 teaspoons salt

GARNISH
1 large carrot
¼ daikon
5 cm (2 inches)
ginger, very
finely sliced

---

1. Rinse the fish under cold water and then pat dry with paper towels. Place the lemon slices inside the fish cavities. Finely grate the ginger over a plate using the smallest side of a metal grater or, alternatively, use a Japanese wooden or ceramic ginger grater. Use your hands to squeeze out as much juice as possible from the pulp. Reserve the juice and discard the dry pulp.

2. Combine the ginger juice, mirin and soy sauce in a small bowl. Lightly brush some of the mixture over fish and sprinkle the sides of each fish with about ¼ teaspoon salt. Sprinkle a thicker coating of salt onto the fins and tail (this will help to prevent them burning).

3. Line the grill tray with aluminium foil and position it to the level furthest away from heat — cooking the fish too close to

the heat will cause them to cook too quickly and they may burn. Cook the fish until golden-brown on both sides, taking care that they do not burn (this will take about 6–8 minutes, depending on the thickness and variety of the fish — the fish is cooked when the flesh flakes easily when tested with a fork).

4. Finely grate carrot and daikon in longish strips using the thick side of a cheese grater; arrange the strips on a serving platter with the sliced ginger. Place the fish on the platter; garnish with some of the ginger slices; serve immediately with steamed rice, if desired. Decorate eye socket with a fresh herb sprig, if you wish.
Note: As the eyes of fish are unappealing when cooked, ask the fishmonger to remove them when scaling and cleaning.

Carefully place the lemon slices inside the fish cavity.

Use a metal, wooden or ceramic grater to finely grate the fresh ginger over a plate.

Sprinkle a thick layer of salt over the fins and tail of the fish.

Finely grate the carrot and daikon radish into long strips.

Fried Pork and Noodles

Preparation time:
25 minutes
Total cooking time:
15 minutes
Serves 4

---

*1 tablespoon
vegetable oil
150 g (4³/4 oz) pork
loin, cut into
small strips
5 spring onions, cut
into short lengths
1 medium carrot,
peeled, cut into
thin strips
200 g (6¹/2 oz)
Chinese cabbage,
shredded
500 g (1 lb)
Hokkien noodles,
gently pulled apart
to separate*

*2 tablespoons water
2 tablespoons
Japanese soy
sauce
1 tablespoon
Worcestershire
sauce
1 tablespoon mirin
2 teaspoons caster
sugar
1 cup (90 g/3 oz)
bean sprouts,
scraggly thin
end removed
1 sheet toasted nori,
cut into fine,
thin shreds*

---

1. Heat the oil in a large deep pan or wok over medium heat. Stir-fry the pork, spring onions and the carrot for 1–2 minutes, or until the pork just changes colour. Take care not to overcook the mixture or the pork will toughen and the vegetables will become limp.

2. Add the cabbage, noodles, water, soy sauce, Worcestershire sauce, mirin and sugar. Cover the wok or pan and cook for 1 minute. Add the bean sprouts and use two large metal spoons or spatulas to coat vegetables and noodles in the sauce. Serve immediately, sprinkled with the shredded nori.

Note: Noodles play a large part in the Japanese diet. Chinese-style thick wheat noodles (Hokkien) are readily available.

Use a large sharp knife to finely shred the Chinese cabbage.

Use your fingers to remove the scraggly end from the bean sprouts.

Stir-fry the pork, spring onions and carrot until the pork just changes colour.

Carefully toss the vegetables and noodles in the sauce.

Shabu-Shabu (Braised Beef and Vegetable Steamboat)

Preparation time:
50 minutes +
30 minutes
refrigeration
Total cooking time:
30 minutes
Serves 4

750 g (1½ lb) scotch
fillet, partially
frozen
15 spring onions,
outer skin removed
3 medium-long thin
carrots, peeled
400 g (12⅔ oz)
button mushrooms
½ Chinese cabbage

150 g (4¾ oz) firm
tofu
8 cups (2 litres) light
chicken stock
sesame seed sauce
(page 33) or
purchased Shabu-
Shabu sauce,
to serve

1. Cut the fillet into thin slices and set aside. Cut the firm section of the spring onions into 4 cm (1¾ inch) lengths and discard the green tops. Slice the carrots. Trim the stems from the mushroom caps, or leave stems on and slice the whole mushroom, if preferred. Chop the cabbage into bite-sized pieces, and discard any tough pieces. Dice the tofu into bite-sized cubes.

2. Arrange the prepared vegetables and the tofu and meat in separate piles on a serving platter, cover with plastic wrap and refrigerate until about 30 minutes before cooking time.

3. Set the table with individual place settings, each with a serving bowl, a bowl of sesame seed sauce, a bowl of rice, chopsticks, soup spoons (if desired) and napkins. Position the food platters and

a cooking vessel (use an electric wok, frying pan or casserole on a burner, or a steamboat) so it is within easy reach of each guest.

4. When all the guests are seated, pour the stock into the cooking vessel, cover with a lid and bring to a simmer. Each guest picks up an ingredient or two with their chopsticks, and places it in the simmering stock for about a minute, or until just cooked. The food is then dipped in the sesame seed sauce and eaten with rice. Serve the remaining stock as soup at end of meal, if desired.

Note: Dashi, made from instant dashi powder or grains, can be substituted for chicken stock. Care needs to be taken not to overcook this dish — vegetables should be just tender and steak still pink in the centre. Prepared sesame seed sauce is available from Asian food stores.

Use a sharp knife to cut the partially frozen scotch fillet steak into thin slices.

Trim the stalks from the button mushroom caps if leaving the caps whole.

Using a sharp knife, cut the tofu into bite-sized cubes.

Arrange the vegetables, tofu and meat attractively on a serving plate.

Soy and Ginger Dipping Sauce

Preparation time:
10 minutes
Total cooking time:
nil
Serves 4

Finely grate the very fresh ginger.

1 cup (250 ml/ 8 fl oz) Japanese soy sauce	*5 cm (2 inches) very fresh ginger, peeled and finely grated* *2 teaspoons caster sugar*

1. Combine soy sauce, ginger and caster sugar in a small bowl. Whisk well and serve within 15 minutes of preparation.

Combine the soy sauce, ginger and sugar in bowl.

Rice

In Japan, nearly every meal ends with a bowl of nutritious rice.

Preparation time:
5 minutes
Total cooking time:
20 minutes +
15 minutes
standing time
Serves 4–6

2 cups (440 g/ 14 oz) short-grain (calrose) rice	*2¹/₂ cups (600 ml/ 20 fl oz) cold water*

1. Place the rice in a sieve and wash well under cold running water. Alternatively, place the rice in a bowl, cover with water, then drain; repeat this process several times until the water runs clear.
2. Add drained rice to a large heavy-based pan and add the cold water. Bring to boil, cover with a tight fitting lid and reduce heat to low. Simmer for 15 minutes, then turn the heat up to high for 30 seconds. Remove the pan from heat and set aside for 15 minutes. Do not remove lid until ready to serve (the steam build-up is essential in the cooking process).

Rinse the rice thoroughly in cold water.

From left: Sesame Seed Dipping Sauce, Soy and Ginger Dipping Sauce, Rice.

Sesame Seed Dipping Sauce

Preparation time:
20 minutes
Total cooking time:
nil
Serves 4

---

100 g (3¹/₃ oz) white
sesame seeds
2 teaspoons light
vegetable oil
¹/₂ cup (125 ml/
4 fl oz) Japanese
soy sauce

2 tablespoons mirin
3 teaspoons caster
sugar
¹/₂ cup (80 g/2¹/₃ oz)
dashi
1 cup (250 ml/8 fl oz)
water

---

1. Roast the sesame seeds in a dry frying pan over low heat for 3–5 minutes, constantly shaking the pan until the seeds are golden brown. Crush the roasted seeds to a paste using a mortar and pestle or a clean coffee grinder. Add the vegetable oil only if necessary, to assist in forming a paste.
2. Mix the paste with the soy sauce, mirin, caster sugar, dashi (or ¹/₂ teaspoon dashi grains in water) and water. Store, covered, in the refrigerator and use within 2 days.

Crush sesame seeds with a mortar and pestle.

33

Marinated Steamed Sake Chicken

Tender and tasty.

Preparation time:
25 minutes +
30–40 minutes
marinating
Total cooking time:
15–20 minutes
Serves 4

---

*500 g (1 lb) chicken
breasts, with the
skin on
1 teaspoon salt
1/3 cup (80 ml/
2³/4 fl oz) sake
2 tablespoons lemon
juice
4 cm (1¹/2 inches)
fresh ginger, peeled,
cut into very fine
matchsticks*

SAUCE
*2 tablespoons
Japanese soy sauce
1 tablespoon mirin
1 teaspoon sesame oil
1 spring onion, sliced*

GARNISH
*2 spring onions
1/2 small red
capsicum*

---

1. Use a fork to prick the skin on the chicken in several places. Place chicken, skin-side-up, in a shallow dish; sprinkle with the salt. Combine sake, lemon juice and ginger in a small bowl; pour over the chicken and marinate for 30–40 minutes.

2. To make Sauce: Combine the soy, mirin, sesame oil and spring onion in a small bowl; set aside.

3. To make Garnish: Peel the outside layer from the spring onions, then cut finely into diagonal pieces. Lay the capsicum flat on a board, skin-side-down. Holding a knife in a horizontal position, cut just under the membrane surface to remove the top layer; discard top layer. Cut capsicum into very fine 3 cm (1¹/4 inch) strips.

4. Line the base of a bamboo or metal steamer with baking paper. Arrange the chicken, skin-side-up, in steamer. Fill a wok or frying pan with 2 cups of water; sit the steamer in the pan. Cover, cook over gently boiling water 15–20 minutes, or until chicken is cooked.

5. Cut the chicken into bite-sized pieces (remove skin if you prefer); arrange in the centre of a serving plate and drizzle with soy sauce mixture. Arrange capsicum strips in a bundle on the side of serving dish, scatter spring onions over chicken. Serve warm or cold, with rice, if desired.

Note: You may use any steamer, or sit a trivet in the base of a frying pan and top with a dinner plate. Arrange the chicken in a single layer on plate, pour about 2 cm (³/4 inch) of water into pan, then cover, and cook.

Use a fork to prick the skin of the chicken breast generously.

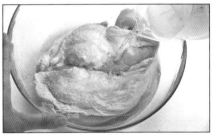

Pour the combined sake, lemon juice and ginger over the chicken.

Use a knife to carefully separate the top membrane layer from the capsicum flesh.

Steam the chicken for 15–20 minutes, or until cooked.

Steak in Roasted Sesame Seed Marinade

Preparation time:
25 minutes +
30 minutes
marinating
Total cooking time:
8–12 minutes
Serves 4

---

2 tablespoons sesame
  seeds
1 clove garlic, crushed
3 cm (1¼ inches)
  ginger, peeled
  and grated
2 tablespoons
  Japanese soy sauce
1 tablespoon sake
1 teaspoon caster
  sugar
500 g (1 lb) scotch
  fillet, cut into
  4 steaks
1 tablespoon light
  vegetable oil

DIPPING SAUCE
3 spring onions,
  outside layer
  removed
4 cm (1½ inches)
  ginger, peeled
½ teaspoon shichimi
  togarashi
½ cup (125 ml/
  4 fl oz) Japanese
  soy sauce
2 teaspoons powdered
  or granulated
  instant dashi stock
2 tablespoons water

---

1. Roast sesame seeds in a dry frying pan for 2 minutes, shaking pan constantly, over medium to low heat until the seeds begin to pop. Place the roasted seeds in a mortar and pestle or in a clean coffee grinder and crush.
2. Combine the crushed sesame seeds, garlic, ginger, soy sauce, sake and caster sugar in a bowl and whisk until the sugar has dissolved. Place steaks in a shallow dish. Spoon marinade over the top of the steaks and set aside for about 30 minutes.
3. To make Dipping Sauce: Thinly slice the spring onions and ginger lengthways, and then cut into fine matchsticks about 4 cm (1½ inches) long. Place the spring onions in a bowl of iced water and leave them until they are crisp and curled. Place the ginger, shichimi togarashi, soy sauce, dashi and water in a small bowl and whisk lightly until well combined.
4. Lightly brush the oil over the steaks and then grill or pan-fry them for about 4–6 minutes on each side—don't overcook them or the steaks will be very tough. Set the steaks aside for 5 minutes before cutting them into diagonal slices. Arrange the slices on serving plates and then drizzle with a little of the dipping sauce. Garnish with the drained curls of spring onion and serve with steamed rice and the remaining dipping sauce.

Use a mortar and pestle to crush the roasted sesame seeds.

Spoon the marinade over the top of the steaks, and set aside for 30 minutes.

Slice the spring onion and ginger finely, then cut into matchstick lengths.

Set the meat aside briefly, and then use a sharp knife to cut it into diagonal slices.

Chilled Soba Noodles

Preparation time:
25 minutes
Total cooking time:
15 minutes
Serves 4

---

250 g (8 oz) dried
  soba (buckwheat)
  noodles
4 cm (1¹/2 inches)
  ginger, peeled
1 medium carrot,
  peeled
4 spring onions,
  outside layer
  removed

SAUCE
1¹/2 cups (375 ml/
  12 fl oz) instant
  dashi stock

¹/2 cup (125 ml/
  4 fl oz) Japanese
  soy sauce
¹/3 cup (80 ml/
  2³/4 fl oz) mirin
good pinch each salt
  and pepper

GARNISH
pickled ginger
thinly sliced pickled
  daikon
1 sheet toasted
  nori

---

1. Add the noodles to a large pan of boiling water. When the water returns to the boil, pour in 1 cup of cold water. Bring water back to the boil and cook the noodles for about 2–3 minutes or until just tender when tested, taking care not to overcook. Drain the noodles in a colander and then cool them under cold running water. Drain thoroughly and set aside.

2. Slice the ginger and carrot into thin slices, then slice into fine matchsticks about 3¹/2 cm (1¹/4 inches) long. Slice the spring onions very finely. Bring a small pan of water to the boil, then add the ginger, carrot and spring onions. Blanch for about 30 seconds; drain and place in a bowl of iced water to cool. Drain again when the vegetables are cool.

3. To make Sauce: Combine the dashi, soy sauce, mirin, salt and pepper in a small pan. Bring to the boil, then cool completely. When ready to serve, pour into four small, wide dipping bowls.

4. Gently toss the cooled noodles and vegetables to combine. Arrange in individual serving bowls.

5. To make Garnish: Use scissors to cut the nori into thin strips; garnish noodles with strips. Place a little pickled ginger and shredded daikon on the side of each plate. Serve with dipping sauce. The noodles should be dipped into the sauce before being eaten.

Note: Soba noodles, made from buckwheat, are like wholemeal noodles but have a unique texture. They are served cold with a dipping sauce as well as in hot soup.

Add 1 cup of cold water after the water returns to the boil.

Slice the carrots and ginger into thin matchsticks; finely chop spring onions.

Place the drained vegetables into a bowl of iced water.

Combine the dashi, soy sauce, mirin and seasoning in a small pan.

Mushrooms in a Spring Onion Dressing

Preparation time:
15 minutes
Total cooking time:
nil
Serves 4

---

2 cm (³/4 inch)
ginger, peeled
500 g (1 lb) button
mushrooms
6 spring onions,
outside layer
removed

¹/4 cup (60 ml/
2 fl oz) Japanese
rice wine vinegar
¹/4 cup (60 ml/
2 fl oz) Japanese
soy sauce
2 tablespoons mirin

---

1. Cut the ginger into very thin slices, cover with iced water to just moisten; set aside.

2. Wipe mushrooms with damp paper towels; trim stalks. Slice spring onions finely, including most of the green tops. Combine mushrooms and onions in a bowl.

3. Combine vinegar, soy sauce, mirin and salt to taste. Pour over mushroom mixture; toss to coat. Set aside 15 minutes. Remove mushrooms and onions with a slotted spoon, draining excess liquid. Arrange on a platter; scatter with ginger slices.

Cut the ginger into very thin slices and place in iced water, to moisten.

Wipe the mushrooms with a damp paper towel to remove any grit.

Pour the combined mixture over the mushrooms and toss gently to coat.

Use a slotted spoon to remove and drain the mushrooms.

Rice Balls

Salmon-filled balls.

Preparation time:
50 minutes
Total cooking time:
2 minutes
Serves 4–6

**2 teaspoons black
sesame seeds
50 g (1²/3 oz) smoked
salmon, chopped
2 tablespoons finely
chopped pickled
ginger**

**2 spring onions,
peeled, finely
chopped
4 cups (740 g/1¹/2 lb)
cooked short-grain
white rice, still
warm**

---

1. Dry roast the sesame seeds in a frying pan over low heat, constantly shaking the pan, for 1–2 minutes, or until seeds begin to pop. **2.** Combine the salmon, ginger and spring onion in a small bowl. Using wet hands, form ¹/3 cup rice into a ball; push 2 teaspoonsful of the salmon mixture into centre of rice and re-form a ball around it. Repeat with the remaining rice and salmon; keep hands wet to prevent rice from becoming sticky. **3.** Arrange the balls on a serving platter and sprinkle with the sesame seeds.

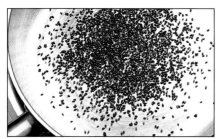

Roast the sesame seeds for 1–2 minutes until the seeds begin to pop.

Combine the salmon, ginger and spring onions in a bowl.

While shaping the rice into small balls, keep your hands wet.

Push 2 teaspoonsful of the salmon into the rice, and then form a ball around it.

Use a mortar and pestle to crush the roasted sesame seeds.

Slice the meat into thin strips, cutting across the natural grain of the meat.

KOREAN

Rustic in character, Korean cuisine has many delicious dishes to choose from — and this selection includes some of the classics.

Barbecued Beef

Popular dish for all beef-lovers.

Preparation time:
15 minutes +
30 minutes freezing
+ 2 hours marinating
Total cooking time:
15 minutes
Serves 4–6

---

500 g (1 lb) scotch fillet or sirloin steak
1/4 cup (40 g/1 1/3 oz) sesame seeds
1/2 cup (125 ml/ 4 fl oz) soy sauce

2 cloves garlic, finely chopped
3 spring onions, finely chopped
1 tablespoon sesame oil
1 tablespoon oil

---

1. Freeze the steak for 30 minutes. Cook the sesame seeds in a dry pan over medium heat for 3–4 minutes, shaking the pan gently, until seeds are nutty brown; remove from pan. Crush in a food mill or with a mortar and pestle.

2. Slice meat into thin strips, cutting across the natural grain.

3. Combine the steak, soy sauce, chopped garlic, spring onions and half the sesame seeds; mix well; marinate for 2 hours.

4. Combine the oils and brush onto a cast-iron grill-plate, heavy-based frying pan or barbecue plate. Heat to very hot and cook the meat in 3 batches, searing each side for about 1 minute (don't overcook or steak will be chewy). Brush and reheat grill between batches. Sprinkle with extra crushed sesame seeds. Serve with Kim Chi (page 46).

Combine the steak, soy sauce, garlic, spring onions and half the sesame seeds.

Sear the meat on both sides for about 1 minute, taking care not to overcook it.

Kim Chi

A traditional pickle.

Preparation time:
9 days
Total cooking time:
nil
Makes about 3 cups

---

*1 large Chinese
cabbage
1/2 cup (160 g/5 1/4 oz)
rock salt
1/2 teaspoon cayenne
pepper
5 spring onions,
finely chopped
2 cloves garlic, finely
chopped*

*5 cm (2 inches)
ginger, grated
3 teaspoons to
3 tablespoons
chopped fresh chilli
(see Note)
1 tablespoon caster
sugar
2 1/2 cups (600 ml/
20 fl oz) cold water*

---

1. Cut the cabbage in half, then into large bite-sized pieces. Place a layer of cabbage in a large bowl and sprinkle with a little salt. Continue with layers of cabbage and salt, finishing with a salt layer. Cover with an upside-down dinner plate that will fit as snugly as possible on top of the cabbage. Weigh down the plate with cans or a small brick and leave the bowl in a cool place for 5 days.

2. Remove weights and plate, pour off any liquid, then rinse the cabbage well under cold running water. Squeeze out any excess water and combine the cabbage with the cayenne pepper, spring onions, garlic, ginger, chilli and sugar. Mix well to combine before spooning the cabbage into a large sterilised jar. Pour the water over top and seal with a tight-fitting lid. Refrigerate for 3–4 days before eating.

Note: Kim Chi is an accompaniment eaten with Korean main meals and with steamed rice. For authentic flavour, use 3 tablespoons of chilli. Bottled chilli paste can be used instead of fresh chilli.

Place layers of cabbage pieces and salt in a large bowl.

Cover the bowl with a plate and weigh down the plate with some cans.

Use your hands to squeeze any excess water from the cabbage.

Combine the cabbage with the cayenne, spring onions, garlic, chilli and sugar.

Fried Noodles

For the noodle-lover.

Preparation time:
30 minutes
Total cooking time:
25 minutes
Serves 4

*¼ cup (40 g/1⅓ oz)
sesame seeds
2 tablespoons oil
2 teaspoons sesame
oil
4 spring onions,
chopped
2 cloves garlic, finely
chopped
2 teaspoons finely
chopped red chilli
150 g (4¾ oz) raw
prawn meat, rinsed*

*150 g (4¾ oz) fresh
firm tofu, diced
100 g (3⅓ oz)
button mushrooms,
thinly sliced
1 red capsicum, cut
into thin strips
2 tablespoons water
2 tablespoons soy
sauce
2 teaspoons sugar
300 g (9⅔ oz)
packet Hokkien
noodles*

1. Roast the sesame seeds in a frying pan over medium heat for 3–4 minutes, shaking the pan gently, until seeds are a nutty brown. Remove from pan at once. Crush in a food mill or with a mortar and pestle.

2. Combine oil and sesame oil in a small bowl and pour about half into a wok or a large heavy-based frying pan. Heat over medium-high heat. Stir-fry onions, garlic, chilli and prawn meat for 2 minutes; remove from pan and set aside. Stir-fry tofu, tossing occasionally until lightly golden, then remove from pan and set aside. Add the remaining oil to pan and add vegetables; stir-fry for 3 minutes or until just crisp.

3. Add water, soy sauce, sugar and noodles to pan. Toss gently to separate and coat noodles in liquid. Cover, steam for 5 minutes; toss well. Add prawns and tofu; toss for 3 minutes over medium heat. Sprinkle with crushed sesame seeds; serve.

Stir-fry the onions, garlic and prawn meat over medium heat.

Stir-fry the tofu, tossing occasionally, until lightly golden, then set aside.

Add the water, soy sauce, sugar and noodles to the pan.

Gently toss to separate and coat the noodles in the liquid.

Cooked Vegetable Salad

Preparation time:
45 minutes
Total cooking time:
15 minutes
Serves 4

---

1 small turnip, peeled, cut into fine strips
2 teaspoons salt
2 tablespoons sesame oil
1 tablespoon oil
2 cloves garlic, finely chopped
1 large onion, thinly sliced into rings
2 sticks celery, sliced
200 g (6¹/2 oz) button mushrooms, sliced
1 large carrot, cut into fine strips
¹/2 red capsicum, cut into fine strips

4 spring onions, chopped

DRESSING
¹/4 cup (60 ml/ 2 fl oz) soy sauce
1 tablespoon white vinegar
3 cm (1¹/4 inches) fresh ginger, very finely sliced and cut into fine strips
1–2 teaspoons soft brown sugar
¹/2 cup (80 g/2²/3 oz) toasted pine nuts, to garnish

1. Place the turnip on a plate lined with a paper towel. Sprinkle with salt, and then set aside for at least 20 minutes. Rinse under cold water; pat dry with paper towels.
2. Heat oils in a large frying pan or wok. Stir-fry the garlic, turnip and onion for 3 minutes over medium heat until lightly golden. Add remaining vegetables, toss well, cover and steam for 1 minute. Remove vegetables from the wok and set aside to cool.
3. **To make Dressing:** Combine the soy sauce, vinegar, ginger and sugar in a bowl.
4. Pour dressing over cooled vegetables and toss. Arrange on a serving plate, sprinkle with pine nuts. Serve with steamed rice, if you like.

Place the turnip strips on a plate lined with a paper towel; sprinkle with salt.

Rinse the turnip strips thoroughly and pat dry with paper towels.

Stir-fry the garlic, turnip and onion for 3 minutes over medium heat.

Combine the soy sauce, vinegar, ginger and sugar in a bowl.

Meat Dumpling Soup

Preparation time:
45 minutes
Total cooking time:
35 minutes
Serves 4–6

---

1 tablespoon sesame
seeds
2 tablespoons oil
2 cloves garlic, finely
chopped
150 g (4¾ oz) lean
pork mince
200 g (6½ oz) lean
beef mince
⅓ cup (80 ml/
2¾ fl oz) water
200 g (6½ oz) finely
shredded Chinese
cabbage
100 g (3⅓ oz) bean
sprouts, chopped,
with scraggly
tail removed

100 g (3⅓ oz)
mushrooms, finely
chopped
3 spring onions,
finely chopped
150 g (4¾ oz) round
won ton pastry
wrappers

SOUP
2.5 litres beef stock
2 tablespoons soy
sauce
3 cm (1¼ inches)
ginger, very finely
sliced
4 spring onions,
chopped

---

1. Roast the sesame seeds in a dry pan over medium heat for 3–4 minutes, shaking the pan gently, until the seeds are nutty brown. Remove at once to prevent burning. Crush in a food mill or with a mortar and pestle.
2. Heat the oil in a pan. Cook the garlic and mince over medium heat until the meat changes colour, breaking up any lumps with a fork. Add the water, cabbage, sprouts, and mushrooms. Cook, stirring occasionally, for 5–6 minutes or until water evaporates and vegetables soften.

Add the spring onions, crushed seeds and season with salt and pepper; set aside.
3. Work with one won ton wrapper at a time and keep the extra wrappers covered with a damp tea towel. Place 1 teaspoonful of filling on a wrapper just off-centre and gently smooth out the filling a little. Brush the edges with a little water and fold over the filling to form a semicircle. Press the edges together to seal. Repeat with the extra wrappers and filling.
4. To make Soup: Combine stock, soy sauce, ginger and half the spring onions in a large pan; bring to the boil and simmer for 15 minutes.
5. Drop the dumplings into the soup and cook gently for 5 minutes, or until they change colour and look plump. Garnish with the remaining spring onions and serve at once.

As the mince cooks, break up any lumps of meat with a fork.

Place 1 teaspoonful of the filling onto the won ton wrapper, just off-centre.

Fold the wrapper over the filling to form a semicircle, then press edges together.

Drop the dumplings into the simmering soup and cook gently.

Shredded Potato Pancake

Preparation time:
25 minutes
Total cooking time:
30 minutes
Makes about 18

DIPPING SAUCE
2 teaspoons sesame seeds
2 cloves garlic, finely chopped
2 spring onions, very finely sliced
1/4 cup (60 ml/ 2 fl oz) soy sauce
1 tablespoon white wine
1 tablespoon sesame oil

2 teaspoons caster sugar
1 teaspoon chopped fresh red chilli

500 g (1 lb) potatoes
1 large onion, very finely chopped
2 eggs, beaten
2 tablespoons cornflour
1/4 cup (60 ml/ 2 fl oz) oil

---

1. To make Dipping Sauce: Dry-roast the sesame seeds in a frying pan, shaking the pan regularly, for 3–4 minutes over low heat, or until the seeds are golden brown. Remove from the pan to prevent burning and let cool for 5 minutes. Combine with the garlic, spring onions, soy sauce, white wine, sesame oil, caster sugar and chilli. Mix well and then place in a serving bowl.

2. Peel the potatoes and grate them on the coarse side of a grater. Place in a large bowl with the onion, eggs, cornflour and season with salt and pepper, to taste. Stir very well, making certain that the cornflour is mixed in thoroughly.

3. Heat the oil in a large heavy-based frying pan (an electric frying pan is good for this). Using 2 spoons drop about 1 rounded tablespoon of mixture onto the hot surface, spread out gently with the back of a spoon so the pancake is about 6 cm (2 1/2 inches) in size. Cook for 2–3 minutes or until golden brown. Cook 4–5 pancakes, or as many as you can fit in the pan at one time. Turn over with an egg slice and cook another 2 minutes on the other side. Do not have the pan too hot or the pancakes will burn and not cook through. Keep the pancakes warm in a very slow 120°C (250°F/Gas 1/2) oven, while cooking the remaining pancakes.

4. Serve with the sauce as a snack or with rice and pickled cabbage (Kim Chi) as part of a meal.

Note: Have all the ingredients ready before potatoes are grated as they will discolour quickly.

Grate the peeled potatoes on the coarse side of a grater.

Drop rounded tablespoonsful of the mixture onto the hot surface.

Make the pancakes about 6 cm (2^1/$_2$ inches) in diameter.

Use an egg slice to turn the pancakes over to cook the other side.

Cellophane Noodles with Stir-fried Beef and Vegetables

Preparation time:
40 minutes
Total cooking time:
25 minutes
Serves 4

---

150 g (4¾ oz)
cellophane noodles
8 dried Chinese
mushrooms
1 tablespoon sesame
seeds
150 g (4¾ oz)
sirloin steak,
partially frozen
4 cloves garlic, finely
chopped
2 tablespoons soy
sauce

2 tablespoons water
2 teaspoons sesame
oil
1–2 teaspoons fresh
chopped red chilli
1 large carrot
½ medium red
capsicum
75 g (2½ oz)
asparagus
2 tablespoons oil
6 spring onions,
thinly sliced

---

1. Place noodles and mushrooms in separate bowls with enough warm water to cover; soak for 20–30 minutes, or until soft. Dry roast the sesame seeds in a small frying pan over medium heat, shaking the pan constantly, for 3–4 minutes or until a nutty brown. Remove from the pan or the seeds will burn. **2.** Slice the steak into very thin slivers, cutting across the natural grain of the meat. Combine with garlic, soy sauce, water, sesame oil and chilli; marinate for 15 minutes. Peel carrot, remove membrane and seeds from the capsicum, and trim the tough ends from asparagus. Cut vegetables into thin strips about 4 cm (1½ inches) long.

Drain the noodles and mushrooms, retaining 2 tablespoons of the mushroom liquid. Finely slice the mushrooms and discard the hard stem. Mix mushrooms with the meat; drain off any liquid and set aside. **3.** Heat a wok or large heavy-based frying pan over medium heat until very hot. Add a little oil; stir-fry meat and mushroom mixture in 2 batches. Sear meat quickly, but do not overcook; remove from pan. Add a little oil; stir-fry vegetables for 2 minutes, then cover with a lid and steam for 1 minute, or until just softened. Add the noodles, reserved liquid and spring onions; toss well. Return meat to pan; cover and steam for 1 minute. **4.** Divide noodles between 4 serving bowls, sprinkle with sesame seeds; serve with extra soy sauce and sesame oil.

Place the mushrooms and noodles in separate bowls and soak in hot water.

Slice the steak into very thin slivers, cutting across the natural grain.

Carefully break off the tough ends of the asparagus spears.

Quickly stir-fry the beef and mushroom mixture, taking care not to overcook.

Potato Noodles with Vegetables

Preparation time:
25 minutes
Total cooking time:
25 minutes
Serves 4

---

300 g (9²/₃ oz) potato starch noodles
4 tablespoons dried cloud-ear fungus
¼ cup (60 ml/ 2 fl oz) sesame oil
2 tablespoons vegetable oil
3 cloves garlic, finely chopped
4 cm (1¹/₂ inches) ginger, grated
2 spring onions, finely chopped
2 carrots, cut into 4 cm (1¹/₂ inch) matchsticks

2 spring onions, extra, cut into 4 cm (1¹/₂ inch) pieces
500 g (1 lb) baby bok choy or 250 g (8 oz) English spinach, roughly chopped
¼ cup (60 ml/ 2 fl oz) Japanese soy sauce
2 tablespoons mirin
1 teaspoon sugar
2 tablespoons sesame seed and seaweed sprinkle

---

1. Cook the potato noodles in a large pot of boiling water for about 5 minutes, or until the noodles are translucent. Drain and rinse thoroughly under cold running water until the noodles are cold (this will also remove any excess starch). Use scissors to roughly chop the noodles into lengths of about 14 cm (6 inches) — this will make them easy to eat with chopsticks. Pour hot water over the cloud-ear fungus and soak them for about 10 minutes.

2. Heat 1 tablespoon of the sesame oil with the vegetable oil in a large heavy-based pan or wok. Cook the garlic, ginger and finely chopped spring onions for 3 minutes over medium heat, stirring regularly. Add the carrots and stir-fry for 1 minute. Add the cooled drained noodles, extra spring onions, bok choy, remaining sesame oil, soy sauce, mirin and sugar. Toss well to coat the noodles with the sauce. Cover and cook over low heat for 2 minutes. Add the fungus, then cover and cook for 2 minutes further. Sprinkle with the sesame seed and seaweed sprinkle and serve immediately.

Note: You may find that potato starch noodles are also called Korean pasta. Cloud-ear fungus is a delicately flavoured dried mushroom — when re-hydrated, they triple in size. Both Korean pasta and cloud-ear fungus are readily available from Asian food speciality stores.

Cook the potato noodles in a large pot of boiling water.

Use scissors to roughly chop the noodles into 14 cm (6 inch) lengths.

Cook the garlic, ginger and finely chopped spring onions for 3 minutes.

Add the noodles, spring onions, bok choy, sesame oil, soy, mirin and sugar.

Spareribs with Sesame Seeds

Preparation time:
30 minutes
Total cooking time:
1 hour
Serves 4–6

---

*1 kg (2 lb) pork
spareribs, cut into
3 cm (1¼ inch)
pieces
1 tablespoon sesame
seeds
2 tablespoons oil
2 spring onions,
finely chopped
4 cm (1½ inches)
ginger, grated*

*3 cloves garlic, finely
chopped
2 tablespoons caster
sugar
2 tablespoons rice wine
1 tablespoon soy sauce
2 teaspoons sesame
oil
1¼ cups (315 ml/
10 fl oz) hot water
2 teaspoons cornflour*

---

1. Trim the pork of excess fat. Dry-roast the sesame seeds in a frying pan, shaking the pan regularly, for 3–4 minutes over low heat, or until the seeds are golden brown. Crush in a food mill or with a mortar and pestle.
2. Heat the oil in a heavy-based frying pan. Brown the spareribs, turning regularly, over high heat until dark golden brown. Drain any excess oil from the pan. Add half the sesame seeds, spring onion, ginger, garlic, sugar, rice wine, soy sauce, sesame oil and water; stir well to evenly coat the ribs. Bring to the boil over medium heat, then cover and simmer 45–50 minutes, stirring occasionally.
3. Combine cornflour with a little cold water and mix to a smooth paste. Add to the pan, stirring constantly, until mixture boils and thickens. Sprinkle with the extra sesame seeds. Serve with steamed rice and Kim Chi (page 46).
Note: Make sure the rib pieces can be held with chopsticks—if necessary, cut them into smaller pieces.

Dry-fry the sesame seeds in a pan until they turn golden brown.

Brown the spareribs, turning regularly, until dark golden.

Add the sauce to the pan and stir well to combine with the ribs.

Combine the cornflour with a little cold water to make a smooth paste.

Binatok (Pea and Rice Pancakes with Vegetables)

Preparation time:
30 minutes
Total cooking time:
50 minutes
*Serves 4–6, makes
approximately 15*

---

200 g (6¹/2 oz) dried
split green peas
100 g (3¹/3 oz) short-
grain rice
¹/2 cup (60 g/2 oz)
plain flour
2 eggs, beaten
1 cup (250 ml/
8 fl oz) water
1 medium carrot
¹/2 green capsicum
¹/2 red capsicum
6 spring onions
3 cm (1¹/4 inches)
ginger
2 cloves garlic

2 teaspoons soy sauce
2 tablespoons
vegetable oil
1 tablespoon sesame
oil
finely sliced spring
onions, to garnish

SAUCE
2 spring onions, very
finely chopped
¹/4 cup (60 ml/
2 fl oz) soy sauce
2 tablespoons water
2 teaspoons sesame oil

---

1. Wash peas and rice in a colander under cold running water until water runs clear. Pour peas and rice into a pan, cover with cold water and bring to boil. Cook for 25 minutes, adding more water if necessary, or until the peas are very soft. Cool, then purée in a food processor.

Add flour, eggs and most of the water; pulse until a smooth batter forms, adding more water until the mixture is a thick pouring consistency. (You may need more than 1 cup of water.)
2. Peel carrot, remove membrane and seeds from capsicum, trim spring onions. Cut

these vegetables into fine matchsticks about 3 cm (1¹/2 inches) long. Finely grate the ginger and chop the garlic. Pour batter into a bowl; stir in vegetables, ginger, garlic and soy sauce.
3. Heat a heavy-based pan over medium heat and, when hot, brush with a little vegetable oil and sesame oil. Pour in 2 tablespoons of batter; cook for 3–5 minutes. When base is cooked, gently run an egg slice around bottom of pancake to release from pan. Turn pancake over, cook other side 2 minutes. Cover pan for about 30 seconds to ensure pancake is cooked, then place on a plate; keep warm in very slow oven while other pancakes cook.
4. **To make Sauce:** Combine spring onions, soy sauce, water and oil in a bowl; mix well.
5. Scatter pancakes with spring onions; serve with the sauce.

Cool the peas and rice, then purée in a food processor until smooth.

Using a sharp knife, cut the vegetables into very fine matchstick lengths.

Pour 2 tablespoonsful of the batter onto the hot surface.

Very gently turn the pancake and cook for a further 2 minutes.

INDEX